Master Em

Intelligence

The Best How-To Guide to
Improve Your Emotional and
Social Skills

By
Mark Sharpe

The trademarks that are used are without any consent, and the publication of the trademark is without permission or backing by the trademark owner. All trademarks and brands within this book are for clarifying purposes only and are owned by the owners themselves, not affiliated with this document.

Table of Contents

Introduction

Human beings are deeply emotional. For a long time, we have valued reason more than what we feel because we saw everything emotional as a sign of weakness.

Thanks to research in this area, it has been proven that our emotions are an essential part of life, as they condition not only our responses but the way we see the events we live and even our decision making (although we have been made to think otherwise).

It is from this turn in the world of psychology that more and more people and corporate organizations have become aware of the need to manage emotions as part of our life transit.

Therefore, learning how to improve your emotional intelligence is recommended in the face of the upheaval and acceleration in which we find ourselves today.

An emotionally intelligent person is characterized because:

- Knows how to recognize how he feels.
- They can identify other people's emotions to understand their own.
- Learns to listen to understand others.
- Connects with people.
- They make humor their lifeline.

Chapter 1. Emotional Intelligence: What It Is and Why It Matters

Emotional intelligence has been one of the latest talking points in corporate America ever since the launch of Daniel Goldman's 1st edition in 1995. For example, whenever an article on the subject was issued by the Harvard Business Review 2 years ago, it gained a high audience than any other article released within this publication in the past 40 years. He was really amazed when the CEO of Johnson & Johnson read that article which he got prints sent to the company's 400 top officers throughout.

It is necessary for IO mental health professionals to identify what it actually means and to be conscious of the research and principle on which it is focused, despite that emotional intelligence is so common in corporate America, and also given that term is a psychological one.

So, I would like to briefly explain the origin of the definition as a field of study in my study journey and discuss how it has become to be portrayed and assessed. I can also point to some of the studies that correlate emotional intelligence with important workplace results, such as individual achievement and organizational performance.

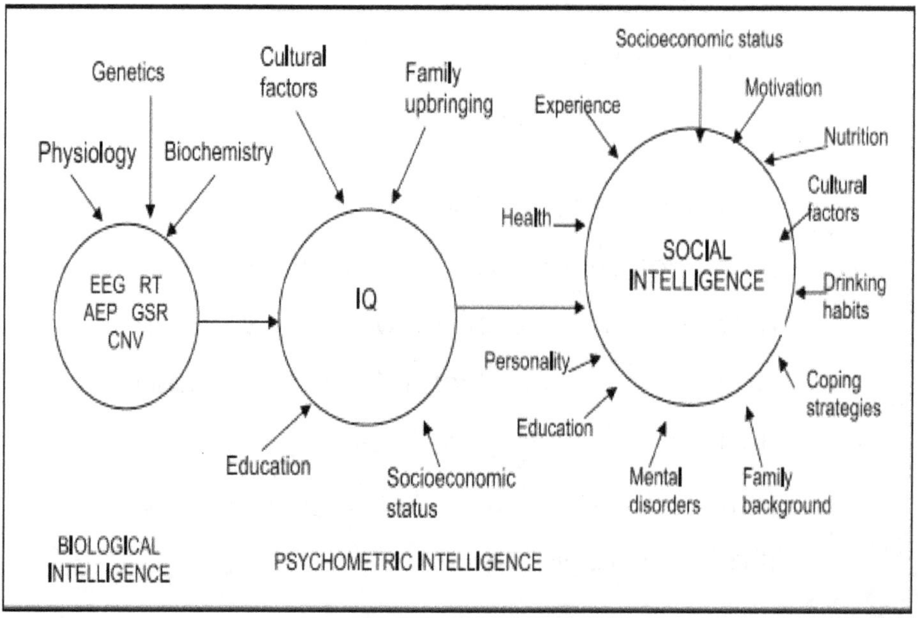

While many leaders in the field have misappropriated and exploited the concept, I believe it stands on a solid scientific framework. Also, though there are elements of the description that are not modern, several components are. After this, emotional intelligence is a direction in which IO psychologists in the field will make highly interesting improvements to their audiences. So, let's start with a bit of history.

1.1. Historical Roots of the Topic

They concentrated on cognitive components, like memories and dilemma, when psychologists started writing and reading about intelligence. There were scholars, even so, who realized earlier that the non-cognitive factors were essential. For example, David Wechsler described intelligence as the individual's overall or global ability to act consciously, think clearly, and cope more effectively with their community (Wechsler, 1958, p. 7).

He applied to both non-intellective and intellectual aspects as early as 1940 (Wechsler, 1940), meaning effective, personal, and social variables. In addition, as early as 1943, Wechsler suggested that non-intellectual skills are important to predict one's capabilities to attain in life. He has also written:

The key concern is whether as variables of general intelligence, non-intellective, that is, effective and conative skills, are admissible.

My assertion was that not only are certain conditions admissible but also required. I have attempted to prove that there are also specific non-intellective dimensions that assess insightful behavior in addition to academic ones. If the above findings are right, it continues that before our studies also provide any assessments of the non-intellective factors, we should not claim to assess overall intelligence [Wechsler, 1943 #316, p. 103].

Wechsler was not the first to see non-cognitive aspects of intelligence as important for growth and development. To give an extreme example, in the late 1930s, Robert Thorndike published a book on intellectual ability (Thorndike & Stein, 1937). Unsurprisingly, until Howard Gardner began writing about diverse intelligence in 1983 when Gardner (1983) stated that intrapersonal and interpersonal intelligence is just as important as the form of intelligence typically measured by IQ and similar actions, the work of these pioneers was generally overlooked or underestimated.

Let us now turn our historical gaze to IO psychology. Under the direction of Hemphill (1959), the Ohio State Leadership Research in the 1940s found that concern was an essential feature of successful leadership. This study found that community leaders who are able to build shared respect, trust, and a sense of comfort and relationship with their constituents are more productive (Fleishman & Harris, 1962).

Around the same time, the Dept. of Strategic Services (1948) founded an appraisal method that included the measuring system of non-cognitive and cognitive skills, based on Murray's earlier work (1938). This method evolved into an appraisal center that was first seen in the private sector by AT&T in 1956. (Bray, 1976). Many social and emotional abilities, such as communication, awareness, initiative, and leadership skills, were and are assessed in appraisal centers (Gowing, in press; Thornton & Bayham, 1982).

I could cite other findings as well as hypothesis strands, but I believe it is self-evident that there has been a long history of research on the role of non-cognitive influences in assisting individuals in both life and the workplace since the early 1990s. This framework is based on the current emotional intelligence research.

Chapter 2: Focusing on Your Habits

This chapter will provide detailed information which all touches upon the area of Emotions and Focusing on your Habits.

There are about a few real needs of living, but for all of us, it really doesn't feel the same way. A lifespan of habits, incorporated by repetition, will actually make us servants to our own brain, a master who is not always helpful.

When your mind processes over your emotions, nothing could be more disturbing or frustrating than criticizing your self-worth, challenging your skills, overbearing you with addictions, or seeking to dictate your actions. If you have ever found, physically or socially, anything compels you to go to places that you don't want to be? Can you feel yourself doing something that you just don't want to do in odd ways?

The explanation is simple: with misleading brain signals; you have trespassed into your subconscious and taken control of your life. If left to its own devices, your brain will lead you to believe false information and behave in a range of self-destructive areas, which include:

- Stuck or panicked by irrational worries and doubts.
- Overthinking situations and worried about something out of your grasp.
- Trapped or distressed by irrational worries and doubts.
- Overthinking situations and worried about something out of your grasp.
- Trying to engage in unhealthy actions to avoid life's regular pressures.
- Reverting to past trends when trying to make a transition.

More and more times you indulge in these toxic habits, the further your brain discovers that your life is based on what is just a habit (a learned behavior). Your brain doesn't decide when the action is helpful or harmful; it merely responds to how you respond and then produces strong emotions, feelings, impulses, appetite, and demands that compel you to continue doing what else you're doing. Regrettably, as often as not, these habits are not those that change your life.

The brain obviously has a firm hold over one's personality, but only if you let it. The positive news is that you can conquer the brain's power by trying to dispel the myths that it has been so effective in selling you by opting to behave in safe, adaptive ways and reconfigure your brain to function for you. That is the goal of this book and the core of our approach: to share our creative, inspiring way of learning how to understand and demystify misleading brain messages so that you build healthy, resilient neural pathways that enable you to live a satisfying life free from these unwelcome, ineffective, and fake trespassers.

It'll be your one, the path you have selected, in the brain you have shaped, not the old course of disturbing acts and habits forced on you by manipulative brain messages.

How is it possible to do this? With our Four-Step process, which provides easy skills and extends to every unsatisfactory aspect of your life, you could use and implement every day. The effect would be a permanent shift of viewpoint, courtesy of a source severely stifled by the misleading brain messages: your wise, loving inner guide. In distorted brain signals, this companion will help you overcome and behave in compliance with your own ambitions, beliefs, and desires. After that, you will see who you genuinely are for the rest of your life, and whatever your brain has convinced you that you are, and bring your true self in the center of the lane.

Is it a challenging goal to achieve? You won't believe that without hearing the accounts of others who have followed our Four Stage approach to turn their lives around. Like Sarah, who suffered depression and self-doubt; Ed, who was crippled by feelings of failure; Steve, who relieved stress with alcohol; Liz, who wondered about her future; Kara, who thought she was updatable because she was ungrateful; Steve, who relieved stress with alcohol; Although the case may not be as drastic or serious, any sort of misleading brain signals impact nearly everyone at some stage of life.

And if our lives are normally calm, when we're anxious or depressed, these misleading thoughts and negative habits figure out a way to slip in and wreak havoc. They have the power to shake our confidence, cause us to pursue ways to escape reality, such as using drugs and alcohol, overeating, wasting money we don't have, ignoring those we care about, getting frustrated, forming unrealistic expectations about ourselves, forgetting to articulate what we really feel or think, restricting our variety of perceptions, and worrying constantly. Yeah, you're naming it.

Except in the most benign lesions, succumbing to misleading brain signals loss time that could be better used elsewhere. At worse, we end up behaving impulsively and in ways that are not reflective of who we truly are, slipping into sorrow and remorse.

Perhaps warmly, when we concentrate on the underlying, unifying source of your distress: misleading brain signals, this effective approach will help you define and cope with the bulk of your problems, not just one symptom. In short, "You Are Not the Brain" can motivate you to take just four quickly mastered steps to approach the ups and downs expertly. Throughout the Four Stages, you'll learn that repetition will change your life and your brain, inspiring you to become the person you want to be.

Change Your Brain Wiring in Healthy, Adaptive Ways in Four Steps

The Four Steps' aim is to show you how to direct your focus because then your brain is reassembled in a balanced, optimistic way. How is it that we know this is occurring? We've done UCLA studies already and seen that in people with obsessive-compulsive syndrome.

Focused on our firm conviction that the mind will alter the brain, we invited participants with OCD to engage in a research project that they either received medication or studied our Four Stage approach to coping with the disruptive, negative experiences they were overwhelmed with on a regular basis. Our staff scanned people's brains before therapy and ten to twelve weeks after they practiced our procedure or took drugs. We were ecstatic to find that those who used our Four Stage strategy experienced the same beneficial improvements in their minds as those who take OCD drugs. Due to the power of our minds to modify our minds, these remarkable brain shifts have happened.

Our results have been supported by recent studies in Germany, which is promising. The study discovered that when they only listened to an audio CD that outlined our mode of therapy, the problems of OCD patients reduced dramatically. That requires to be reiterated because it is crucial to the direction you are about to start on: by pursuing the Four Steps, these participants were offered no other treatments, only an audio CD, their commitment, and their attempt at making improvement.

2.1. The Four Steps

Step 1: RELIABLE

Identify the misleading brain's signals and the uncomfortable feelings by calling them what they are.

Step 2: REFRAME

Contextualize your view of the relevance of misleading brain signals; explain why these emotions, desires, and impulses appear to annoy you: they are fake brain signals (It's not ME, it's only my BRAIN!).

Step 3: REFOCUS

Concentrate your energy on a positive and constructive task or mental operation, even if misleading and manipulative desires, impulses, feelings, and experiences are still active and bothering you.

Step 4: REVALUE

Acknowledge your emotions, desires, and impulses for what they are: all sensations induced by false brain signals of little to no significance (they are something to dismiss, not focus on).

In our Four Stage approach, you can learn how to center your mind in positive ways, much as these people did, so you can retrain your brain while improving and inspiring your true self at the same time.

2.2. Why Is It So Difficult to Maintain Healthy Habits?

It seems to be extremely simple to fall into bad habits.

- Intake of junk food
- Lying in front of the TV rather than going to the gym.
- Having to go to a job you dread every day.
- Biting the ends of your fingernails.
- Tobacco use.

There is no shortage of behaviors that are toxic and unmotivated. So we're all involved with them from beginning to end.

So why is that? You deserve to lead a life that is healthy, satisfying, and exceptional. Every now and then and, you'll be truly inspired and motivated to make a change. So, what leads you to think you'll are doing the same thing next year, except this time with something better health? Why is this so difficult to keep good habits?

I think it's because we often choose to go in a reverse way. And in this segment, I'll provide a smarter strategy for making long-term changes in your life based on a mixture of research and real experiences.

Get this session started.

The Widely Known Screw-Up You Should Avoid

Modifications and everyday successes draw a lot of attention. (Who doesn't want to be more successful in much less time for a good reason?)

So here's the issue: whenever you hear about a dramatic transformation (including someone reducing 100 pounds) or an exceptional great accomplishment (such as someone launching a million-dollar company in a year), everything you know is all about the present case. You wouldn't understand enough about the process that followed it or the trends that led to the ultimate result.

It's easy to be seduced by these amazing tales doing far too much, too soon. I'm pretty. Actually, I did. It's all too tempting to get concerned with the results when you're ecstatic to bring your look to the next level. I want to lose 20 pounds (or 40 or 60 or 100). I require 300 pounds to drop (or 400 or 500). I'm positive I ought to breathe deeply three days a week (or five or seven) or dozens of other variations of your life priorities. It's rational to believe that we require the effect, the transition, and the success of the evening. You, on the other hand, may not need it. You should build healthy habits.

It's all too tempting to exaggerate the magnitude of a particularly key time, while the importance of creating good decisions on a daily basis is undervalued.

Every other habit, positive or evil, evolves as a result of those small decisions over time. Even if this is so if today's issues are the outcome of thousands of small choices taken over time, it may seem strange that the path to success, health, power, satisfaction, satisfaction, meaning, and endurance is made up of a large number of daily decisions, but how easily we forget this when trying to make a change.

When you're concentrating on achieving a goal quickly, you lose track of the idea that how we attain our results is almost as important as whether or not we accomplish them in every direction. The desire to achieve success easily deceives you into assuming that the end product is the reward.

On the other side, the truth is here...

And become exactly the sort of person you want to be is really about the regular processes you follow than that of the end outcome you accomplish; somebody who holds oneself to a higher standard believes in themselves and can be assured by others who relate to them.

Whatever makes you think this is real? In fact, your present life is the total value of your habits. Will you be in decent physical health or otherwise? Your habits have made you a suspect.

How pleased or sad are you? As a result of the routines.

Why successful or inefficient are you? You are a victim of your routines.

Anything you do on a constant schedule (i.e., all you care about it and do) has an effect on where you're from, your values, and the impression you project.

The most frequent mistake people make is focused on an upcoming case, transformation, or success rather than their own routines and rituals.

That's the same act for which everybody involved has been found guilty. And, like others, I'm always on the lookout for new attempts to modify my habits.

Nonetheless, through time, I've acquired a powerful blend of genuine life knowledge and academic practice, which has helped me in a number of fields. Throughout this section, I'd want to discuss my experience with you so how you can focus on your lengthy objectives rather than aiming for the next achievement right away.

Let's start with the notion of establishing and preserving good habits.

2.3. Functioning of Habits (The Change of Habit 3 R's)

Every habit is a basic three-step procedure. That's what I call the "3 R's of Habit Change," which functions the way...

1. **Reminder** (the trigger that initiates the behavior)

2. **Routine** (the behavior itself; the action you take)

3. **Reward** (the benefit you gain from doing the behavior)

Duhigg points to the three phases as prompt, ritual, and opportunity in his book. Irrespective of how this is formulated, the argument is there is a lot of science throughout the extent of habit-forming, so we can be pretty sure that habits pursue the very same process.

Let me explain to you what the 3 R sounds like in real life by adding the form to a common habit. (Throughout this case, reply to a phone call.)

Phase 1: The very first step is that your phone is ringing. This is a clear indication that generates the action. The ring serves as a reminder or a cue to tell you to take a call. That request is the baseline for action.

Phase 2: Pick up the phone. That's where the real play is moving. Must get into the habit of responding when the call sounds.

Phase 3: You're trying to find out who's trying to get in touch. The incentive is the profit of doing the deeds. Throughout this case, the reason to fulfill the habit was to fulfill the desire to figure out why you have been named by other individuals.

Result: This chain is a constructive chain of affirmation if the incentive is positive, which reminds the mind, "Are doing the same way every night this prompt happens" (i.e., When the phone rings again, answer it).

Do this process a couple of times until you should avoid worrying about it? Your behavior is potentially going to become a habit.

In much the same 3-step process, all behaviors are formed.

Where are you using this method to develop and maintain new habits? Here's how it is.

Step 1: Using a Current Habit as a Reminder for the New One

When you talk to your colleagues about forming a new habit, they will inform you that you'll have to maintain your personality or start a different medication of strength.

I continue to reject it.

Being worried about trying to remember a new move is the complete opposite of getting on with life. It sounds like you're talking about it. You always feel motivated, and then you shouldn't, right? Why can you keep relying on imagination to form a new habit (something you want to commit to) (one which changes)?

This why the warning, which serves as a catalyst for new behavior, is such a topic of the great importance of creating new habits. Instead of focusing on being inspired, a great reminder makes it simple to continue your activity by turning your fresh concept into what you actually do.

To begin with, I created a new habit of dental floss every day after brushing my teeth. Brushing my tooth was a routine I always had, and it served as a stimulus or trigger for my new habits.

I purchased a bowl, set it beside my toothbrush, and filled it with a few before the flosses to keep everything much smoother and stop having to remember where I take the mouthwash. Any time I look for my toothpaste, I also see floss.

This was much easier to change by posting a noticeable alert and relating my regular framework to current actions. There's no need to be encouraged. There's no reason to recall anything.

How to Pick a Reminder

It just doesn't depend even if you're going out, eating well, or painting art; you can't expect yourself to commit to a new routine without first having a framework that makes it easy to continue. As a consequence, determining the right cause for your lifelong routine is the very first move in making the change smoother.

This same prompt you use to initiate your new behavior is incredibly important to your existence and the pattern you are attempting to create.

I've noticed that having two lists is the most efficient method of informing yourself of your most current habit. Create a record of the stuff you do each day, without fail, in the very first checklist.

Consider the following scenario:

- Take a shower.
- Pull your shoes on.
- Brushing your teeth is a must.
- Ensure that the toilet is clean by rinsing it.
- Take a seat at the table for dinner.
- Switch off the lights.
- Relax on the bed.

Any of these items are commonplace beauty practices, such as washing your hands, consuming tea in the morning, brushing your hair, and so on. These approaches may function as a signal for new lifestyle behaviors.

Create the main record of all that occurs to you on a regular basis.

- You come to a full halt at a red light.
- You've got a text message.

- On air, there is an ad.
- An album came to a close.
- Sunsets are stunning.

These tasks may also serve as prompts for one's everyday actions. "For example, when an advertisement appears on the television, I do five sit-ups," she says.

For some of the above list, you are already doing and already reacting to it every day; you will get a wide range of topics. For routine tasks, these are the great markers.

In addition to being an inspiration, let's assume you want to feel energized. Yet feeling grateful is another established way of improving satisfaction. You should use the "sit down for lunch" note from the first list as a catalyst to confront the truth you're grateful for lately.

"There's one thing I claim as I sit down for lunch that I'm thankful for today."

That's the kind of little gesture that can lead to a more thankful attitude toward life in general.

Step 2: Make Your Habits Incredibly Easy to Start

As I described at the start of this section, it's very easy to sweep up in need to make big lifestyle changes. We are looking at impressive weight loss outcomes and accept that we have to lose 40 pounds within the next four weeks. We can see good players on Television and think we can run further and climb higher every day.

Those are my thoughts as well, so I understand. And I, in general, respect passion. I'm glad you need to have wonderful things in your life, and I want to do what I can to help you do them. But, even after changes, it's significant to mention that long-term success is part of everyday activities.

If you'd like to develop a new lifestyle and live a better and stronger life, I have one piece of advice that I can't stress quite so: start tiny. "Take into account it extremely relevant that you can't say no," suggests Leo Babauta.

What inconsequential do you believe it's really? As per Stanford Professor BJ Fogg, individuals who would like to start brushing must begin by exfoliating just one tooth. There's just one.

Performance would not make a big difference at the start. What cares is that you are the sort of person who still meets the new timetable, even no matter how trivial or meaningless it might seem to be. If the behavior has become more consistent, you will indeed be able to achieve the level of success you desire.

Some recommendations: Begin a fresh habit that you want to develop. Now it's up to you to decide: "Why would I find this particular initiative so easy that I won't be able to say no?"

Step 3: Always Offer Yourself a Compliment

Meant to honor is expected. (It holds true in life, as well as in actions, in my view.)

When it comes to sticking to good practices, there is an intrinsic motivation to continue to improve ourselves by continuing to do things that make us all feel comfortable.

As a consequence, it's important to value yourselves once you develop a new habit.

For context, if I'm focusing on a new exercise goal, I'll still remind myself, "It was a fantastic day," or "Good day," at the end of a session. You've made strides today.

Then you'd even tell yourself, "Big win!" anytime you looked like it. "Keep it to yourself.

As an option, "Growth! Progress!" Now will be the best time to develop a new habit.

Given the fact where I have done anything on my own, several people are motivated.

- Front tooth floss. "Success! Victory! "
- Eat a nice, nutritious diet. "Yay! Success! "
- Do seven pushups. "Nice job!"

If you're not used to empowering yourself with positive self-talk, it will take some time to get used to it. However, amid its irony, a study has shown that the reward is an important part of the habit-forming process. Give yourself kudos and delight in some little win.

Essential note: Make sure you understand the patterns you're attempting to build. When you're really doing something, it's tough to find a benefit, but you hope someone will expect it or agree with you. It's your life; just make sure you spend it on things that matter to you.

Let's talk about how to shape habits in real life now that we have looked at the fundamentals of habit-forming.

How to Build Long-Lasting Routines Based on Your Identity

The easiest way to set up prolonged procedures is to first focus on developing a different ethnicity. Your present actions are just a snapshot of your identity at the moment. What you're doing right now is an inverted version of the sort of person you imagine you'll become, either rightly or wrongly.

To transform your behavior for the better, you must begin to believe in new self-perceptions.

Consider how we generally set goals.

"I'd just want to lose some weight," or "I need to be bigger and healthier" might be the starting point. If you're lucky, somebody might say, "Indeed, that is fantastic"; you, on the other side, need to be more effective.

After that, you suggest, "I'd like to start losing 15 pounds" or "I'd like to lose 200 pounds."

These targets are based on our results or our personalities.

Performance and attitude expectations are perfect because they're close to behaviors. If you're undertaking an operation, it will assist you in achieving different goals. However, if you're beginning a new activity, I agree that starting with a character target will be much more effective.

The difference in priorities depending on race and goals based on performance and personality can be seen in the figure below.

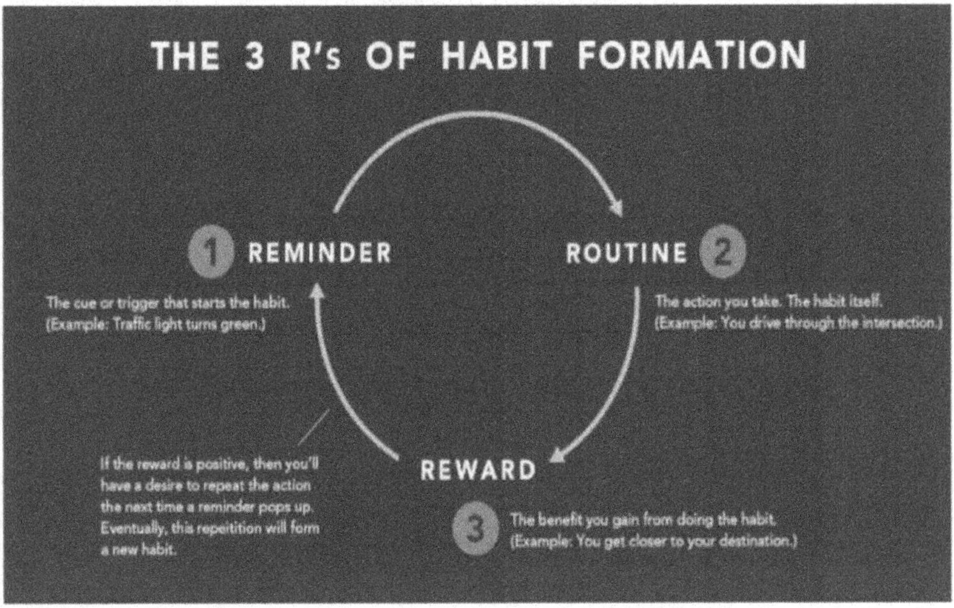

Your personality is characterized by an internal shift in actions and the production of good behaviors. Any action you take is inspired by the idea that anything is possible. Once you transform your attitude (the kind of person you believe you are), it will help you to adjust your acts.

The explanation's so difficult to commit to new patterns is that we all want to reach an objective focused on success or appearance without changing our identity. Before demonstrating to ourselves that we've had the persona about the kind of character we would like to portray, we aim for perfection in many ways.

It should be done in a precise way.

2.4. The Key to Long-Term Success

Changing your mind isn't as tough as you would think. There are two stages that can be accessed.

1. Make a decision on the kind of person you want to be.

2. Show minor victories to yourself.

Note: I cannot emphasize more how crucial it is to keep taking little steps. The goal is to become the type of person who can accomplish those goals, never to just get the result instantly.

A person who has worked out regularly, for practice, is the kind of individual who would gain stamina. Develop the personality of someone who starts with the fundamentals and then goes on to success and presentation. Start tiny and believe that when you grow a new identity, the outcomes will follow.

Over the next section, you'll find five real-world explanations of how to implement identity-based patterns.

Sample 1: Do you want to shed a few pounds?

Identity: Being the kind of person that travels more each day.

Purchase a pedometer for a small victory. When you're done, take 50 steps away from your desk. Tomorrow, take 100 steps. The next day, there will be 150 moves. At the completion of the first year, if you're doing the five days a week and add 50 footsteps per day, you'll have walked over 10,000 footsteps a day.

Sample 2: Do you want to be the next great author?

Becoming the kind of man that produces 1,000 words a day is my identity.

Stunning win: Write one report every day this week.

Sample 3: Do you want to be a strong person?

Becoming the kind of man who never loses an exercise is my identity.

You do pull-ups on Mondays, Wednesdays, and Fridays, which is a slight triumph.

Sample 4: Do you want to be a better friend?

Becoming the same kind of person that retains contact with others.

Small victory: Dial one friend every Sunday. If they replay the same individuals every three months, you'll keep in contact with twelve old friends over the course of the year.

Sample 5: Must you get to be treated seriously at the task?

Becoming the kind of person that keeps to their routine.

Narrow victory: Make appointments with a 15-minute break between those them so that you can go from client to client and be on time every time.

What Is Your Real Identity?

In my experience, it is far more vital to affirm your identity to yourself than to gain awesome rewards if you wish to excel at anything. This seems to be particularly true at first sight.

So, if you're trying to be empowered and motivated, watch videos online, hear music, or play games. If you miss working out after a week, don't be discouraged. You can't rely on getting inspired in every life to make big improvements. You have to be the kind of person you want to be, and that begins by announcing your new title.

If you wish to make a lot of difference, I suggest starting thinking about your personality rather than the results. Grow into a person capable of carrying out the tasks you desire. Make it a routine right now. The outcomes can take a long time to appear.

Optimal productivity approaches are being used to tackle the crisis.

Identity-based activities give you a frame of reference for determining your goals. The 3 R's of habit change include a technique for creating your new personality. Incorporating both of these ideas would make development easier for you in the long term.

In other terms, identity-based activities keep you focused on the positive things, such as starting little, establishing your identity, and not worried about the consequences.

Meanwhile, the 3 R's of pattern change guarantee that you do things right, such as linking a new habit to current activity and praising yourself with work well done.

2.5. The Most Efficient Way to Begin Your New Habit

In other sentences, if you're concerned about getting greater than you seem to be now, if you're adamant about committing to good behaviors, you need to take small steps.

The following specific patterns, both positive and poor, can be found: Brushing your teeth is an utter requirement. Make sure you're wearing your safety belt. It's the biting of the nails.

Such behaviors are so trivial that you wouldn't even care about them. They aren't something you do on a daily basis. These are simple gestures that evolve into long-term patterns.

Doesn't it make any sense that the best way to continue forming new habits does be to make minor changes that our brain might quickly learn and replicate?

What about if you began worrying about your goals in life as little, achievable goals that you can accomplish whenever the time is right, even if you have more money, or when you get your major move? Rather than treating them as small, regular habits that must be repeated before performance can be avoided?

Even if it's not dependent on a study getting the correct diet or a tremendous dose of determination to lose 50 pounds, but on a set of minor habits you could still handle? Moving for 15 minutes a day, consuming six glasses of water per day, and taking two instead of 3 meals.

Participants get fixated on making life-altering improvements for even other reasons. I'm hoping you'll make more gains if you focus on your fitness patterns.

Can You See the Differences?

From BJ Fogg, an instructor at Stanford University, I believe this idea is summed up wonderfully.

Whenever you plant the perfect crop in the right place, it will flourish without any additional coaxing. I accept that this is the perfect metaphor for forming patterns.

The "perfect seed" is the tiny activity you select. The only thing that distinguishes the "right place" from the "wrong location" is sequencing. The component of "coaxing" that I agree has nothing to with forming trends is amplifying creativity. In fact, depending on motivation to alter habits is totally incorrect.

And soon as you get a boost of enthusiasm, the standard response is to fall in headfirst, only to lose your balance and wishing you had much more energy as the daily schedule begins to deteriorate. The latest strategy is to dive across shallow water, steadily increasing depth before you reach the point where you can swim to see if you are motivated.

Everyday activities—small, repeatable routines—help you fulfill big dreams. Think big, but start little.

2.6. Allow New Habits a Part of Your Life

One thing is learning how to make improvements, but implementing new aspirations into your life seems to be something different altogether.

It is difficult making improvements. The persistence of life will drag you away from your priorities and straight back through your old routines if your schedule gets wild.

How can you conquer this propensity to go off track and make time in your timetable for fresh objectives?

The 3 R's of behavioral change and identity-based behaviors, as well as other techniques listed in this guide, will help you remain on track.

But the only resources at your side are not such tactics. In this segment, I'll explore another strategy for sticking to healthy behaviors that don't necessitate a lot of courage or encouragement. I'll also offer two instances of how I've effectively applied this technique with my own experience.

What's Wrong with the Way We Normally Set Goals

If you are just like a normal person, so in your life, you have hopes and aspirations. In fact, you actually have a long list of activities that you'd like to complete.

That's fantastic; however, when it falls to goal-setting, people make stupid mistakes. (I know that I have made this mistake myself many times.) The issue is that we defined a target.

We consider the ultimate target we'd like to reach and the timetable we'd like to follow. We say things like, "By the summer, I would like to lose 20 pounds," or "I like to add 50 pounds to my bench press in the next 12 weeks."

The trouble with this strategy is that if we don't adhere to the arbitrary timeline, we built at the onset, we sound like losers. The excellent thing is that there is a better way to do it, and it's easy.

The Strength in Designing a Scheduling System, Not a Timetable

Having a timeline with an order to fulfill rather than a target to meet is, in my opinion, a better way to define good behaviors.

Rather than giving yourself a target (and afterward feeling like a failure if you don't achieve that) to hit a specific strategy, you should choose an objective that is important to you and therefore set a timeline to work consistently toward that.

It does not sound like a big change, but it is.

2.7. In Motion: A Description

Allow me to demonstrate this technique using two concrete examples through my own existence, as I aspire to become a leader of my thoughts rather than simply someone who voices their viewpoint almost all the time.

Example 1: Trying to Write

I publish a new article every Monday and Thursday. I've been delivering two posts a week, every week, from my first post on October 10, 2014.

I didn't always operate on a Monday-Thursday schedule. In fact, I came up with reasons for actively avoiding a schedule. I told myself, *"I do my best writing when I'm inspired, so I'll just wait until I get the urge to write."*

I assumed that if I wasn't doing my best work, then I shouldn't be doing it at all. The problem with that strategy is that my output was erratic at best.

It took me a while to realize it, but it's not about always doing your best work; it's about doing the best you can on a consistent basis.

Once I stopped focusing on results and simply held myself to a consistent schedule, my work and my output improved. In the first six months after I started writing two times per week, I wrote more in quantity and better in quality than in the previous two years.

Example 2: Workout

A few years ago, I set a target of doing 100 press-ups in a row with perfect posture. I just got 36 the first time I tried it.

I may have set a target myself in the past: "Do 100 press-ups by the end of the year."

Each time, I wanted to make an exercise routine. Every Monday, Wednesday, and Friday, I began performing pushup sessions. For any particular exercise, there was no absolute pull-ups target. The main goal is to finish the exercise. (Just like no single target exists for any of the papers I start writing.) The only target is to process it correctly and safely.

I'm already working for 100 consecutive pushups (mine existing best is 80), but in the 30 days before I started, I've maintained my Monday, Wednesday, and Friday routine and done over 100 pull-ups sessions.

Concentrate on the Activity Rather Than the Results

Can you notice how the two cases above vary from the rest of the targets we formulated for ourselves?

I made reasonable strides against my targets in both situations (trying to write and work out) by keeping to a timetable rather than setting deadlines for my results. The emphasis is on carrying out the action rather than fulfilling X's deadline.

Offer yourself a plan to execute, not a timetable to reach, if you'd rather be the kind of individual who actually achieves tasks on a daily basis.

How to Make Big Changes without Overwhelming Yourself

I'm a true believer in taking on one goal at a time. There is indeed a mountain of experimental evidence proving that it is less effective to multi-task and split your attention than to remain dependent on a specific purpose.

And so what if you were to modify some facets of your life? And what if you want more for one thing to be better. And you want to do that right now?

Well, I have wonderful news. You will really concentrate on a single issue when changing your life in several ways at the same time due to "keystone behaviors."

Let's look at what catalyst patterns are or how you can integrate them into your everyday routine.

2.8. The Effect of Keystone Habits

A keystone habit is an action or ritual that puts the rest of your life in balance, naturally.

This definition was first presented to me in Charles Duhigg's book "The Force of Habit." I began to note a few patterns that contributed to positive actions elsewhere as I started looking into my own life.

When I lift weights, for example, something strange happens.

I want to eat healthier while I work out. I feel like eating balanced, unprocessed snacks, although I might reward myself with chocolates and ice cream.

I appear to be more active as I return to work after exercising. My mind is sharper, and crisper is my prose. Feelings come naturally to me.

I still fell asleep easily at the end of the day. When I wake up, I prefer to sleep more and to feel new.

And I have the opposite result when I do not work out. I become more vulnerable to eating fast food. I sit up longer, become more easily distracted, and spend time on unimportant activities. Stress is building, and I am starting to feel pain in my back.

In other words, the keystone habit that holds the remainder of my life in order is exercise. I don't have to worry about being better at feeding. I don't have to push myself to work on finishing assignments.

I'm not really at the top of my game, but it seems to come a bit better on the days I practice something. Naturally, fitness drives me to the best self.

What Are Your Keystone Habits?

It's not nearly as complicated as you would imagine to change your lifestyle and become the kind of person who "gets their act together." Actually, before the dominoes start crashing everywhere, you would need only one keystone habit.

If you have many aspects you want to enhance, consider how much easier it would be for you to achieve if you learned one or two keystone patterns that put you on the track to success automatically.

What's the great news? You probably know what all these habits are for you now.

What is the one thing that makes your day run more smoothly when you do it?

It's worked out again for me. In the meantime, other people swear by racing in the morning. And you'll find hundreds of CEOs who say the secret to their success is their frequent meditation habit.

No longer what your keystone habit is, reflecting on it and doing more of it worth your effort. When exercised regularly, the right habit will have a huge effect on your life.

How to Get Back on Track After Slipping Up

The formation of behaviors depends on the ability to recover fully. And there will be moments where it's practically difficult to execute your daily schedule.

Small hiccups, though, do not make you a loser; they consider you human. Most efficient individuals in the world mess up on their routines too. What distinguishes them is not their capacity to escape accidents; it is their ability to easily get back on the right track.

The crucial thing to remember is that it is not to deter defeat. It is to prepare for it the correct way. You should "prep for uncertainty" using the 4 strategies below and build a method for getting back in shape before you can get off the direction.

1. Put your habits on your calendar.

2. Develop a Plan for Bouncing Back

3. Have someone who expects something of you.

4. Design your environment for success.

Development can be complicated. Your good behaviors can take two steps forward rather than one step back at first. Predicting such losses and devising a method for rapidly getting back on track will help a lot.

2.9. Split a Bad Habit

We have collected a lot of data on how to build healthy habits, so what about breaking poor habits?

Bad practices hinder your life and deter you from fulfilling your objectives. Both psychologically and physically, they hinder your health. They even waste your time and money.

Why are we even doing them, then? And most importantly, will you do something about it? How can you get rid of your bad habits and replace them with healthy ones?

I obviously don't have all the answers, so I'm going to continue reading and share what I've found about how to overcome a bad habit.

What Causes Bad Habits?

Someone's bad habits are often caused by two factors: Sadness and pressure.

Bad habits are just a means of coping with tension and boredom much of the time. A quick reaction to stress and frustration can be anything from biting your nails to underspending on a shopping trip to partying every weekend to wasting time on the internet.

It doesn't have to be away, though. You should teach yourself new and better ways to cope with stress and depression, which you can then replace your unhealthy habits with.

Often hidden difficulties really trigger the tension or frustration that is on the surface. These things may be difficult to worry about, but you have to be honest with yourself if you're serious about making improvements. Are there any convictions or motives behind bad habits? Is there something deeper that triggers you to hang on to is bad for you—a doubt, an occurrence, or a restricting belief?

To resolve them, understanding the roots of your poor habits is essential.

You Don't Break a Bad Habit; You Replace It

All the behavior's that you have right now, positive or evil, are for a cause in your life. These habits favor you in certain respects, even though they are detrimental to you in some ways.

When it comes to drugs or liquor, the advantage is often biochemical. It's emotional frequently, like if you remain in a relationship that's terrible for you. And your poor habit is an easy way to deal with discomfort in certain ways. Biting your nails, dragging your hair, scratching your hip, or clenching your jaw are only a few examples.

Such "benefits" or explanations often refer to smaller bad habits.

Checking your mail account as soon as you switch on your device, for example, can make you feel more linked. Having to look at all of those emails at the same time saps your productivity, splits your concentration, and stresses you out. So it saves you from worrying like you're "dropping out"... and then you're doing it again.

It's impossible to simply break bad habits when they have some kind of gain in your life. (That's why simple suggestions such as "please stop doing it" seldom work.) Alternatively, you ought to swap a bad habit for a new habit that has a comparative advantage.

For context, if you smoke when you get depressed, then when that happens, it's a bad plan to "just quit smoking." Instead of smoking, you would come up with a different approach to cope with depression and adopt the new activity in place of smoking.

If you want yourself to just stop doing bad things before changing them, you'll be left with unmet needs, and it'll be tough to stick to a "please don't do it" regimen for too long.

How to Break a Bad Habit?

Here are few bonus tips for changing your bad habits and thought in a different way about the process.

Make a proposal to replace that unhealthy habit. You must practice ahead of time for how you will act when you are faced with the tension or boredom that causes your bad habit. What are your preparations if you have the need to smoke? (Instead, try deep breathing.) What are you supposed to do when Facebook beckons you to do something you don't want to do? (Example: for a job, write one sentence.) You need to make a roadmap on what you're trying to do rather than your bad habit, whatever, and whatever you're coping with.

Take out as many potential stimuli. If you drink while you smoke, don't go to a pub. If you eat chocolate and they're all in the kitchen, toss them all out. If the first thing you do when you sit down on the sofa is pick up the TV remote, place it in a separate room's wardrobe. Make breaking unhealthy habits easier on yourself by reducing the problems that create them.

Just now, the surroundings make bad habits simpler and healthy deeds more complicated. Adjust the environment, and the result can be modified.

Alternatively, team up with somebody and getaway together. The two should keep each other open and collectively share the successes. It is a strong motivator to realize that everyone else wants you to do successfully.

Envision yourself to meet your goals. Try stopping smoking, consuming nutritious items, or showing up sooner. Whatever the poor habit, imagine yourself smashing it, laughing, and loving your success is that you are striving to crack. See yourself creating a fresh brand.

You don't have to be anyone else; you just have to go back to your old self. We also assume that to destroy our bad habits, we must turn into a totally different human. The fact is that to be somebody without your bad habits, and you still have it in you. It's very doubtful, really, that you've had these bad habits all your life. You don't have to be smoking, and you just have to return to being a non-smoking guy. You don't have to turn into a healthy human; you just have to go back to becoming healthy. You have always existed without this poor habit, even though it was years before, which implies you should do it again.

To resolve negative self-talk, use the phrase "but." One thing about combating bad habits is that punishing yourself for not behaving better is easy. It's quick to remind yourself how bad you suck any time you screw up or run into trouble.

Whenever that happens, finish the sentence with "but."

- *"I'm fat and out of shape, but I could be in shape a few months from now."*
- *"I'm stupid, and nobody respects me, but I'm working to develop a valuable skill."*
- *"I'm a failure, but everybody fails sometimes."*

Create a contingency to lose. Every so often, we all make mistakes. "When you mess up, miss a run, eat bad meals, or sleep in, it doesn't make you a bad person," says my key guy Steve Kamb. It's getting you human. Greetings and welcome aboard."

So, instead of berating yourself for making a mistake, brace for it. What distinguishes top stars from everybody else is that they will get back on course really soon, and we'll all get off track.

Taking the First Step to Breaking Bad Habits

Getting wrapped up in how you behave regarding your bad habits is simple. You may feel shame or waste your time thinking of how you would like things to be. But these theories keep you away from what is really going on.

Alternatively, it's an experience that can teach you how to really make progress. What is that bad habit really going to occur? How often times a day do you do it? Where else are you located? Who are you going out with? What causes the behavior to start, and what causes it to be triggered?

Simply keeping track of these problems would make you more aware of the situation and provide you with a slew of options for coping with it.

Here's an easy way to get started: just watch how many occasions your bad habit arises every day. Put a sheet of paper and a pen in your pocket. Create a note on your notebook any time a bad habit emerges. Add up all the tally points at the end of the day to get the sum.

Your purpose is not to criticize yourself or feel bad for doing anything unhealthy or inefficient at the start. The only purpose is to be mindful of when it does and how frequently it happens. By being conscious of it, wind your mind around the issue. Then you should start putting the tips in this essay into effect to break your bad habit.

It takes time and commitment to break unhealthy habits, but most importantly, it takes persistence. Many people who excel in overcoming their unhealthy habits try and fail numerous times before eventually succeeding. You cannot make progress straight away, but it does not rule out the chance.

Chapter 3: Becoming an Emotionally Intelligent Leader

This chapter will provide detailed information that all touches upon the area of Emotionally Intelligent Leaders and becoming an EI leader.

When it comes to mental maturity, we have the upper hand. That is the most critical element of studying how to take advantage of it. We should both focus on raising and enhancing our EQ.

If you're just getting started, this chapter will provide you with foundational practices such as goal-setting, finding time for personal growth, and meditation for better knowing yourself. The transforming segment is for more senior executives who have more experience. This is where you start measuring, taking stock of your talents, and evaluating how to develop them. You create relationships in this process that catapult your career to new heights.

Although empathy cannot come easily to us in the workplace, it may be precisely what our workers need. This chapter explores ways to resist regressive actions and reinvent ourselves, as well as the catalysts for transformation and how to get started. We will both lock down what we've learned and strive to grow into the leaders we want to be.

First Steps

1. Are you able to put in the time to get to know yourself better than you have before?

2. Are you ready to ask yourself the difficult questions and frankly answer them?

3. Will you go for what you really want, even though it makes you uncomfortable?

I begin with these three questions because the responses are crucial to improving emotional intelligence. If you want to develop your EQ and become a sought-after thought leader, you must first and foremost concentrate on yourself, on the foundations of emotionally intelligent leadership, which begins with self-awareness for a cause. It all starts with self-awareness, with realizing who you are. I give you five ways to get started, as you'll see in the first activity at the end of this chapter.

As previously mentioned, the job starts with you taking time on yourself. If you wish to successfully direct someone, you must first keep your own house in order. I talk of putting a solid framework in place in my executive coaching job. This is what I refer to as the "EQ Game Plan for Leaders."

Self-awareness entails having a good view of your beliefs, passions, meaning, mission, and priorities. You develop the self-confidence and inspiration to evolve into the image of yourself you've dreamed of when you're clear on these things. We should personalize these things for ourselves in the same way that great organizations have a vision, goal, and mission.

Although the game plan would be short, it will be much more difficult to implement than you expect. It necessitates you being absolutely honest with yourself. You must hold yourself to a high level of determination and discipline in order to get to your authentic heart as an individual and leader. You should start setting the foundations for your life and career right here.

Once you've put your system in place, you can start reverse engineering. Begin with the outcomes, not only in your brain but in the paper! Write down precisely what you intend to accomplish—the outcomes for which you are prepared to bring in the effort. Build backward from there to get exactly what you want.

Moving on to a longer-term approach, I highly advocate making a five-year plan for your life. This advice has come from Fortune 500 CEOs, retired millionaires, and well-respected colleagues. It's something I've learned so many times from so many people I value that it's become one of the most valuable characteristics I think a leader can possess.

When you talk and write down your wishes, you achieve an immense amount of strength in your life. All you have to do is take it upon yourself to do it. It really is that plain, but sitting down to do it isn't always easy.

Every strategy is just as successful as the amount of self-sacrifice and action you're able to bring forward. The greatest ideas in the world can come to naught if you are unable to take action. Bear in mind that you'll have to change your tactic. When life changes all around you, you must keep going and making improvements. That is the key to improvement, as well as the key to survival. If you're able to prepare and take action, you will accomplish your goals.

The late coach John Wooden, one of life's great role models, described the achievement as "peace of mind, which is a direct product of self-satisfaction in feeling you put forth the effort to become the best you can be."

Performance is a mentality that necessitates full effort. It's a mental state and a state of mind. Also, self-satisfaction puts a heavy focus on self. The acceptance or appreciation of others can never decide your performance. If that's the case, you're in for a very disappointing life. I implore you to ask yourself, "What will progress look like today?" as you begin each day. When it comes to being a successful leader, one of the first actions you can take is to address this issue.

Visualization gets your juices going and makes you hungry to accomplish your goal when you continue to bring your strategy together. Visualization and creativity work together to stoke the fire that drives your inspiration and resolve. Reciting your proposal aloud has a lot of strength.

Finally, merge confidence with the written and spoken words to tie them together. The rest is all about working out your policy. To push yourself ahead and never look back, you'll need confidence and energy, which comes from knowing you're on the right track.

A philosophical first step is indeed a great one to take. Getting a philosophy of who you want to be and what you want to do is immensely valuable. This is what other people refer to as a personal creed; I refer to it as your personal mission statement. This is a published record that identifies three points:

1. The explanation for your life

2. Your point of view

3. The substance of what is important to you.

Your raison d'être—or why you're doing what you're doing—is the reason you're doing it. This should be normal and produced entirely by you, regardless of any outside factors or emotions.

The acts you must take to meet the criteria of your why are decided by your guide. New leaders sometimes challenge themselves, and they don't feel they're able to start going in the direction of their goals. They feel it is not their moment, that they lack a certain ability, or that they are too young. They're stymied by restricting attitudes that breed distrust and doubt.

It could make sense to start small and work your way up to achieving activities and goals that are important to your purpose. This is where writing down the targets and arranging them into a strategy comes in handy. This is the compass that will lead you when life gets in the way when you're too distracted or exhausted to think straight. It is important to prepare accordingly.

The substance of what matters to you is an important part of the why, and it should be integrated as far as possible into your everyday routines. There are the basic beliefs, morals, principles, people, and things that motivate you to live a life full of energy and excitement.

Now you may compose your mission statement in a simple and concise way. Here's mine: Through my writing, speaking, and coaching, I want to inspire others and make a real difference in their lives, all while enjoying each moment to the fullest and maintaining a good outlook, smile, and sincere joy for life.

Values provide us with a firm base on which to traverse the peaks and valleys we'll face. Honesty, trust, perseverance, empathy, and modesty are some of the virtues that leaders integrate into their arsenal. These are widely acknowledged and useful principles, as well as core elements of leadership, regardless of the environment.

If you asked Steve Jobs what made him perfect, he would tell you that it was his sense of direction, his confidence in himself, his hard work, and his love and passion. That's why, from an all-time epic expression, one of his most memorable quotes is an exhortation to obey your heart. Values are important to good businesspeople, as well as to you and me.

Keep yourself responsible on a weekly basis. On a day where you know you'll be able to concentrate, set aside 30 minutes of quiet time. Examine your mission statement once more. Examine the priorities. Are you succeeding in reaching them? What do you do better if that's not the case? It's crucial to note that it's not only about introducing new things; often, it's just as important to eradicate projects and behaviors that aren't adding value. These first steps set the foundations for the framework you'll need to advance as an emotionally intelligent leader.

3.1. Transforming

The best leadership advice I've ever got is to begin developing partnerships as soon as possible. I'm talking about your personal and professional relationships, as well as your friendship with yourself. We mostly thought about your friendship with yourself in First Steps. You must first look internally and be firm in your principles, plan, and objectives in order to bring meaning to those in your company.

The fundamentals of self-awareness are learned by the changing leader, who then establishes relationships with individuals both within and outside their organization. The transformative leader recognizes that driving transformation and policy necessitates the creation of relational capital, which must be achieved with sensitivity and a sincere willingness to support others.

Relationships are the basis for new prospects, growth, and the attainment of our long-term objectives. We can't do it on our own, no matter how introverted, individualistic, or creative we are.

Consider this: How frequently do we want to make things work without even developing a relationship with others? And how much do you work out like that? Transformative executives can still be in the mentality of trying to know their workers in order to mobilize them and drive them toward reaching strategic objectives. Curiosity, candor, and a desire to contribute are the foundations of true business partnerships.

Developing partnerships assists in the growth of our mental store of knowledge. We learn what will and will not work in this enviroment. Organizational politics, leadership, and history are among the subjects we study. Learning about the company's past, working out what makes people tick, and displaying a sincere desire to help are all critical facets of work success.

Day one is the perfect time to start developing these critical job relationships! Relationships generate substantial compound interest over time, so it's best to get underway as quickly as possible. Building strong partnerships that are personal, honest, and sincere can help you immensely if you work for a startup, hedge fund, food services firm, or ad agency. People will sense phoniness a mile away, and they won't want to support you if you're only using anything to scale the ladder or "cheat the machine."

Transformational leaders are acutely mindful of their workers' desires and are smart enough to change their leadership styles when required. Situational Leadership, created by the late Dr. Paul Hersey and Ken Blanchard, author of the bestselling book "The One-Minute Boss," sets out a structure for how to handle leadership in various circumstances, based on the workers' preparation. Adaptability is at the core of situational leadership. It is focused on transition! Despite the vicissitudes of the sector and the ever-changing competitive world, many companies depend on this system, which is built on years of study. It shows you how to lead based on your employees' preparation level.

Employees deserve to be remembered by their employers. They want to feel like they belong, particularly if it's mirrored in the culture. They like to hear more about their leaders' decision-making skills as well as their personalities. "Across all income groups, the top measure of job success is not paying: It is the organization's culture and values, accompanied closely by the consistency of senior leadership and the company's employment opportunities," says Dr. Andrew Chamberlain, chief economist for Glassdoor. Compensation and benefits are regularly ranked as the least significant indicators of job satisfaction of the six workplace factors studied.

A transformational leader knows that their company's ideals and culture will define its success. They create a meritocracy-style system, recognizing top performers and presenting them with the opportunity to progress to senior leadership roles in the future. They pay attention to their workers' needs, partnering with team partners to adjust success improvement, and stressing the human factor of human resources to keep good people on board. "To be effective, you need to mobilize the resources of many people in your organization," said Dr. Michael D. Watkins, a renowned authority on market transformations. "Your vision, expertise, and motivation will propel you forward and act as seed crystals if you do the right things."

"How did I answer in the face of hardship, adversity, or loss?" question yourself as you focus on your life. When you decide to use pressure in your favor, you'll learn a lot about yourself and make your biggest strides.

A transformative leader is also a transition catalyst, capable of predicting and reacting to change before it occurs. Payal Kadakia, as we learned, was mindful of shifting market preferences about personal fitness. She believed and found that others thought the same way she did when she couldn't find the classes she needed. Kadakia's idea showed that if she designed it, they would come by delivering a service that was in high demand but had never been delivered before.

This is work that we will all do on our own until we find out what the most important facets of our careers are—or, as I like to refer to them, the large rocks. Stuff like meeting your strategic plan's priorities, developing new executives, reaching sales projections, and ensuring you have the best staff in the right places are the big rocks. Transformative executives concentrate on the most critical problems and assign the pebbles to other team members.

It's impossible to speak about change without often considering reinvention. Transforming leaders are never happy—and definitely not complacent—in their technical achievements. They recognize that personal growth (such as coaching, yoga, and reading new books), as well as professional development (such as attending leadership conferences, learning new technologies, and training), are important for them to continue to improve as leaders.

A transforming leader asks for suggestions (or, as we'll talk about in the next session, "feed forward") to help them gauge their success. A transformational leader tries to strengthen all his or her qualities and shortcomings. Transforming leaders are conscious, self-aware, and inspired to make each day their masterpiece while developing new approaches to bring their company forward.

3.2. Common Challenges

Overcoming the illusion that people would take advantage of you if you lead with empathy is a common struggle for someone seeking to become an emotionally intelligent leader. Some people claim that "putting people first" means "people will march all over you." You might have a mental picture of a manager who is bossy, unapproachable, and too focused on the bottom line to engage in discussion. Unfortunately, traditional leaders like this will occur depending on the sector.

Being an emotionally knowledgeable leader isn't a sign of weakness; it's a power that brings people together. "When a leader accepts their duty to care for people instead of accounting for numbers," writes Simon Sinek in Leaders Eat Last, "people will follow, fix challenges, and see to that the leader's vision comes to fruition the right way, a stable way, rather than the expedient way."

Another common obstacle for emotionally intelligent leaders is sharing more intimate knowledge about themselves with others they lead. This is challenging for leaders who are naturally reserved. Opening up to your real self can be tough. It can be difficult to find inspiration for social time if you are more introverted. Instead of treating this social time as a draining thing, think of it as a chance to interact and express yourself with others. When your staff sees more of the real you, anxiety will disappear, and you will be able to communicate with trust.

If you've been a good leader without changing your personality or attempting new positions, you're likely to fail at first. What if you're asked to lead a new department while having no expertise in the field, but you're trusted because of your business acumen? How can you react to learning a new talent, collaborating with new people, and probably depending on others more than you have in the past?

Given how much positions shift—face lets it, some of us change companies every couple of years—having an agile mentality is crucial. It's all too normal for a leader to feel utterly confused when he or she is shifted from one business entity to another. Immerse yourself by talking about different departmental responsibilities and the numerous leadership positions within the organization. Promotional opportunities will emerge if you have a working knowledge of the team's core functions and, of course, have formed crucial relationships with your current department.

So many leaders feel they only need to be competent in one field; this is obsolete thought. Build experience in one field, but "diversify your portfolio" by learning about a range of market functions. It's a win-win scenario for business awareness and key partnership growth. Get yourself at ease with being uncomfortable. Pressure yourself in ways you haven't done before.

A fully adaptable, high-EQ leader is flexible and sensitive to the demands of the market, has a balanced staff, and knows how to better employ your strengths while compensating for your limitations.

3.3. Resisting Regression

It's much easier to return to a negative habit than it is to sustain a healthy one. We know that as emotionally knowledgeable leaders; we have the potential to develop and change. We also realize that it is not easy. It needs time, commitment, and discipline. Unfortunately, plenty of us struggles with some of the foundations of emotional intelligence.

They necessitate our continuous focus and understanding. The most powerful efficiency and time-management advice advise us to shape routines, which means that we should be persistent and dedicated. So, if we're trying to prevent regressive conduct, we need to work with this disciplined mentality.

- Ignoring what we believe to be real because the urgency of the moment pushes us to behave rashly.

- Make a dismissal or promotion decision on the spur of the moment.
- Putting all the blame on ourselves.
- Believing that we should lead by decree, raised voice, or demand, particularly when it isn't an emergency.
- Depriving ourselves of opportunities for contemplation and reinforcing our core self since "we've moved past the basic point."

All the main elements of emotional intelligence are defective in regressive behavior. Since tension, transition, strain, and conditions have rattled you, and you're regressing from the strides you've made. You've returned to short-term thought rather than returning to the base you've created. In short-term thought, strategies take priority over strategy. When we have a plan behind what we do, we are usually the most effective. This necessitates meditation, mindfulness, and a cost-benefit analysis.

Emotionally aware leaders make a deliberate effort to act in a certain manner.

Empathy isn't something that comes easily to anyone, and as a result, it's always the first thing to go as we get more self-centered. Even the most self-motivated leaders may be weighed down by tough splits, business dips, or a defeat to a rival. Decisions are either deferred or taken haphazardly for no rhyme or justification. Often bear in mind that high-EQ leaders have empathy for themselves.

I hope you will handle yourself with compassion, both personally and publicly. Regardless of the winds of transition and emotion, we must make time to be kind to ourselves. This is why it's so vital to be surrounded by people who love and understand us. It is imperative that we be faithful to ourselves at all times. I know you have confidence and ego in secret. I believe the same way. Everyone else does, too! We must never cause our view of how others perceive us to affect how we behave ourselves. Life would be that much happier in the long run if we lead with dignity.

Persistence is the trait that people value the most. This persistence—drive—is what helps one to take the first step and keep going as an emotionally intelligent leader. Persistent correspondence is an art form. Being persistent and striving for our targets every day is an ability. In fact, I'd rather be remembered for my perseverance, demeanor, and work ethic than for my skills. Perhaps you will as well.

We may have all the potential in the world, but it won't matter if we don't put in the time and perseverance every day. Ask yourself, "Can I contribute more each day to being the best version of myself that I can?" no matter where you are in your career. I assume you will discover that the answer is yes. People will look up to you because of that.

A completely self-aware mindset against addition and subtraction is the perfect way to thwart regressive actions. It's what I refer to as "playing offense and defense." The bulk of us invests our time in the offensive zone. We are on the lookout for any potential advantage. We play with different ways to accomplish the same objectives. We engage in workshops to learn new skills. We network and attempt to establish new links. Both of these items are wonderful and have a high monetary impact.

The concern is that until this is followed by a protective mindset—one that insists on removing time-wasters as well as self-destructive thoughts, actions, and behaviors—all the high-value activities would be pointless. People who are emotionally intelligent excel when they think for themselves, understand their emotions, attitudes, and behavior, and then change and adjust their behavior to concentrate on high-value tasks. They get rid of or downgrade tasks and events that don't add much value. There are high-value behaviors that include "playing offense":

- Holding a diary for self-reflection to share your opinions, concerns, and emotions, both socially and professionally.
- Holding a diary for self-reflection to share your opinions, concerns, and emotions, both socially and professionally.
- When preparing and scheduling your weekly time blocks for gatherings, idea generation, and work, you should prioritize starting your day with inspiring reading and videos and seeding in moments for them.
- Imagine yourself meeting your unique expectations and meanings of achievement, imagining what it sounds

like, how it feels, and what it would take to get there.

These are "playing defense" activities:

- Deciding which meetings and activities you should assign.
- Bringing in contingency time for unexpected emergencies or conditions that need your attention.

We must be aware of the words we use, the ideas that invade our heads, and the records we make. Made it a habit to stop making excuses. Excuses result in a loss of ownership, which is a hallmark of those who assigned responsibility to others. Delete explanations from the repertoire when they contribute to procrastination. When we put off things we don't want to do, we're more likely to blame ourselves, lament our lost time, and, in the worst-case scenario, lose sleep and feel heightened tension. Putting off stuff that needs to be done right now is not a winning technique.

Take this "feed-forward" strategy from esteemed coach Marshall Goldsmith, as published in the Harvard Business Review, to better fix regressive behavior:

1. Clarify your objective to everyone you know in a straightforward and concise way.

2. Demanding two recommendations. Encourage imaginative thinking.

3. Pay attention to what's being said. Create a list of your thoughts.

4. Express thanks by saying "thank you." There's nothing left. There will be no excuses or defensiveness.

5. Proceed by enlisting the support of more people.

Any forms of regressive actions that can infiltrate the mind can be combated by cultivating a continually self-improving mindset. Accepting advice and asking for as much support as possible in that field to help you develop is the "feed-forward" part. When you advance as a leader, be constructive and open to new prospects.

Conclusion

Experts agree that this type of intelligence plays a vital role in both personal and professional success, being even more important than IQ. In any case, EQ seems to be linked to everything from decision making to academic performance.

So the question is, what do you need to be emotionally intelligent? Daniel Goleman talks about five critical components of EQ:

1. **Self-awareness**

This is the way we become aware of our emotions and are able to evaluate them. Most of us are so busy with the daily routine that we rarely stop to think about how we are responding to situations and how we are feeling. The other form of self-awareness recognizes the emotions of others toward us.

This is often difficult because we tend to see what we want to see and tend to avoid asking others for opinions if we think they will be uncomfortable for us.

By improving our emotional self-awareness, we may be able to understand many more things in our daily lives. It is also interesting to learn how to gather feedback from people who are honest with us and whose ideas we value.

2. **Self-regulation or emotional self-control**

Self-management is the ability to control our emotions. This also includes emotional transparency, capacity for adaptation, accomplishment and optimism.

People with a good level of self-regulation tend to be flexible and adapt well to change. They may also be skilled at handling conflicts and dealing with tense or challenging situations. Goleman goes on to suggest that people with very strong self-regulation skills stay on track without wandering off course. They are able to positively influence others and take responsibility for their own actions.

3. **Social skills or interpersonal relationships**

This is about being able to interact well with those around us, regardless of the place and situation. True emotional understanding involves more than just understanding our own emotions and the feelings of others; it is also about being able to put this information into practice in our daily interactions and communications.

In professional settings, people with good social skills are able to build good relationships, and connections with co-workers learn how to develop a strong rapport with leaders, peers, and subordinates. Some important soft skills include active listening, verbal communication skills, non-verbal communication skills, leadership and persuasiveness.

4. **Empathy or recognition of others' emotions**

Empathy is the ability to understand the feelings of others; it is absolutely fundamental to EQ. But this involves more than just being able to recognize the emotional states of others. It also involves responding to people based on this information. If we empathically perceive that someone is feeling sad or hopeless, we will be better able to influence the way we respond to their emotions. We will be able to show our concern and make an effort to keep helping them feel better at these times.

Being empathetic also allows people to understand the power dynamics that often influence social relationships, especially in the workplace. Those who have good competence in this area are able to exercise proper influence in relationships, understand how feelings and behaviors work, and effectively interpret the different situations that revolve around these types of power dynamics.

5. **Self-motivation**

Self-motivation also plays a key role in Emotional Intelligence. Emotionally intelligent people are usually motivated over and above mere external rewards, such as reputation, money, or status. They may feel a genuine passion that drives them to fulfill their own internal needs and goals. They seek things that lead to internal rewards and engage in experiences that lead them to feel good about themselves.

Individuals who become skilled in this area tend to be action-oriented. They set themselves goals, are highly driven, have a high need for achievement, and are always looking for ways to do better. They also tend to be highly committed to social issues and are good at taking the initiative to carry out a wide variety of tasks.

CPSIA information can be obtained
at www.ICGtesting.com
Printed in the USA
BVHW071826230621
610293BV00015B/2293

9 781801 568548